Britt,

So many of the pages in this book seem to have a special meaning or phrase that in some way reminds me of you or of "us". I underlined a few things, but there too many to mark.

When you read through this I hope you can be reminded of how much I love you and how very special you are to me. You have so many great qualities and abilities. Everyone around you can see that. I hope you can too!

I love you so much!
mom

Britt,

I want this book to put a smile on your face. I want it to remind you that you have been on my mind. And I want it to help you remember — every time you see it in the days yet to be   that this book was given to you just because... you're very special to me.

Love you - Mom

For You, Just Because
You're
Very Special
to Me

*Thoughts to Share with
a Wonderful Person*

Updated Edition

Douglas Pagels

Blue Mountain Press™
Boulder, Colorado

Library of Congress Control Number: 91-73570
ISBN: 978-1-59842-602-1

▉ and Blue Mountain Press are registered in U.S. Patent and Trademark Office.
Certain trademarks are used under license.

Printed in China.
First printing of this edition: 2011

✪ This book is printed on recycled paper.

This book is printed on paper that has been specially produced to be acid free (neutral pH) and contains no groundwood or unbleached pulp. It conforms with the requirements of the American National Standards Institute, Inc., so as to ensure that this book will last and be enjoyed by future generations.

Blue Mountain Arts, Inc.

P.O. Box 4549, Boulder, Colorado 80306

Contents

Has Anyone Ever Told You This?

Has anyone ever told you what a wonderful person you are?

I hope so! I hope you've been told dozens of times... because you are just amazing.

And just in case you haven't heard
those words in a while,
I want you to hear them now.

You deserve to know that...

It takes someone special to do
what you do. It takes someone rare
and remarkable to make the lives
of everyone around them nicer,
brighter, and more beautiful. It
takes someone who has a big heart
and a caring soul. It takes someone
who's living proof of how precious
a person can be.

It takes someone... just like you.

A Little Story About "You and Me"

Me: So lucky to have this special connection!
You: The wonderful person I'm so thankful for.

Me: Someone who means well, but doesn't always get it right.
You: Someone who gives my life so many smiles and so much encouragement.

Me: A little insecure, a little uncertain, a little crazy sometimes.
You: A huge help and a calming influence... all the time.

You: Know what's going on inside me better than anyone.

Me: There isn't anybody else I can trust like this and no one I feel so comfortable turning to.

You: On a scale of 1 to 10, with 10 being the best, at least a 20.

Me: Counting my blessings and hearing your name come up so many times.

You: A joy to be with, to think of, and just to talk to.

Me: So incredibly glad... there's you.

Twenty Beautiful Things
That Are True About You

You are something — and someone — very special. You really are. No one else in this entire world is exactly like you. You're a one-of-a-kind treasure, uniquely here in this space and time.

You are here to shine in your own wonderful way, sharing your smile in the best way you can and remembering all the while that a little light somewhere makes a brighter light everywhere.

You can — and you do — make a wonderful contribution to this world, and there are so many beautiful things about you.

You have qualities within you that many people would love to have, and those who really and truly know you are so glad that they do...

You have a big heart and a good and sensitive soul. You are gifted with thoughts and ways of seeing things that only special people know. You know that life doesn't always play by the rules but that, in the long run, everything will work out. You understand that you and your actions are capable of turning anything around — and that joys once lost can always be found.

There is a resolve and an inner reserve of strength in you that few ever get to see. You have so many treasures within — those you're only beginning to discover... and all the ones you're already aware of.

Never forget what a treasure you are. That special person in the mirror may not always get to hear all the compliments you so sweetly deserve, but you are so worthy
of such an abundance
...of friendship, joy, and love.

This Is Your Reminder

Every time you glance at this book, whether the day has been pleasant and easy or difficult and demanding, I want this to be your reminder that your presence in the world is always a wonderful thing. You are so deserving of every happiness I can possibly wish, and I constantly find myself thinking of you and wishing you knew about the smiles you inspire.

I want you to come home to these words in all the seasons ahead. And I want you to feel a glow in your heart just from knowing that you never, ever have to wonder if you're in someone's thoughts or if there's anybody out there who truly and lovingly appreciates you, because...

This book is always going to be here to tell you how much... I do.

Do You Know
How Important You Are
to Me?

*I know you probably wonder from time to
   time what you mean to me.*
*So I'd like to share this thought with you, to
   tell you that you mean the world to me.*

*Think of something you couldn't live
   without... and multiply it by a hundred.*

Think of what happiness means to you... and add it to the feeling you get on the best days you've ever had.

Add up all your best feelings and take away all the rest... and what you're left with is exactly how I feel about you.

You matter more to me than you can imagine and much more than I'll ever be able to explain.

Twenty-Four Things to Always Remember... and One Thing to Never Forget

Your presence is a present to the world.
You're unique and one of a kind.
Your life can be what you want it to be.
Take the days just one at a time.

Count your blessings, not your troubles.
You'll make it through whatever comes along.
Within you are so many answers.
Understand, have courage, be strong.

Don't put limits on yourself.
So many dreams are waiting to be realized.
Decisions are too important to leave to chance.
Reach for your peak, your goal, your prize...

Nothing wastes more energy than worrying.
The longer one carries a problem,
   the heavier it gets.
Don't take things too seriously.
Live a life of serenity, not a life of regrets.

Remember that a little love goes a long way.
Remember that a lot... goes forever.
Remember that friendship is a wise investment.
Life's treasures are people... together.

Realize that it's never too late.
Do ordinary things in an extraordinary way.
Have health and hope and happiness.
Take the time to wish upon a star.

And don't ever forget...
for even a day...
how very special you are.

Thoughts I'd Love to Share with You

*You are so important to my days —
and so essential to the smile
    within me.
That certain space where our lives
overlap is the place that brings me
the most understanding,
    the most peace,
the nicest memories, and a joy that
    comes to my heart so constantly.*

Because you're so important to me,
I want your life to be such a wonderful one.
I wish you peace, deep within your soul;
joyfulness in the promise of each new day;
stars to reach for, dreams to come true,
and memories more beautiful
than words can say...

I wish you friends close at heart,
  even over the miles,
and loved ones — the best treasures
  we're blessed with.

I wish you present moments to live in,
  one day at a time;
serenity, with its wisdom;
  courage, with its strength;
and new beginnings, to give life a
  chance to really shine.

I wish you understanding
    of how special you really are
and a journey, safe from the storms and
    warmed by the sun.

I wish you a path to wonderful things;
an invitation to the abundance
    life brings;
and an angel watching over,
    for all the days to come.

For You

I don't know exactly what it is... but there is something very special about you.

It might be all the things I see on the surface: Things that everyone notices and admires about you. Qualities and capabilities. Your wonderful smile, obviously connected to a warm and loving heart. It might be all the things that set you apart from everyone else.

Maybe it's the big things: The way you
never hesitate to go a million miles out
of your way to do what's right. The way
your todays help set the stage for so many
beautiful tomorrows. Or maybe it's the little
things: Words shared heart to heart. An
unspoken understanding. Sharing seasons.
Making some very wonderful memories.
The joys of two people just being on the
same page in each other's history...

If I could ever figure out all the magic that makes you so special, I'd probably find out that it's a combination of all these things — blended together with the best this world has to offer...

Friendship and love, dreams come true, strong feelings, gentle talks, listening...

...laughing and simply knowing someone whose light shines brighter than any star.

You really are amazing.

And I feel very lucky to have been given the gift of knowing how special you are.

You Are So Deserving

You are so deserving of every good thing and every brighter day that could ever be wished.

I hope all the things you long for will find their way into your life.

May the days be good to you: comforting more often than crazy and giving more often than taking.

May the passing seasons make sure that
  any heartaches are replaced with a
  million smiles and that any hard journeys
  eventually turn into nice, easy miles that
  take you everywhere you want to go.

May your dreams do their absolute best to
  come true...

Love, mama

May your heart be filled with the kindness of friends, the caring of everyone you love, and the richness of memories you wouldn't trade for anything.

May life's little worries always stay small.

May you get a little closer every day to any goals you want to achieve.

May any changes be good ones and any challenges turn out to be for the better.

May you find time to do the things you've always wanted to do!

And may you be happy... forever.

Priceless Moments

*I wouldn't trade the days
I've spent with you for anything.*

Well... maybe just one thing.

A million more just like them.

If I Could

If I could have a wish come true, I'd wish for every day of your life to be blessed with some special gift that warms your heart, some wonderful smile that
 touches your soul,
  and so many things that simply
  take your breath away.

I Care So Much About You

*I care about you
    more than I can say.
And that caring and that feeling
have a meaning that is more precious
to me than I can explain.*

But let me try to tell you this...

*Saying "I care" means that I will always
    do everything I can to understand...*

*It means that you can trust me.
It means that you can tell me
    what's wrong.*

It means that I will try to fix what I can,
that I will listen when you need me to hear,
and that — even in your most
   difficult moment —
   all you have to do is say the word,
      and your hand and my hand
         will not be apart.

It means that whenever you speak to me,
whether words are spoken through a smile
   or through a tear...
      I will listen with all my heart.

Hopes and Wishes

These are my hopes and my wishes...
That we may always be more than
close; that nothing will come
between the bond we share.
That I will always be there for you,
as you will be for me.
That we will listen with love.

That we will share truths
  and treasured memories.
That we will trust and talk things out.
That we will understand.

That wherever you go,
  you will be in my heart,
and your hand will be in my hand.

What It Takes

It takes a certain kind of person to be special.

It takes someone who is really wonderful; someone who lights up this little corner of the world with feelings of friendship and love and understanding. It takes a truly unique personality and a knack for making life happier and more rewarding.

It takes someone who's willing to take the time. It takes an individual who is able to open up and share their innermost feelings with another. It takes someone who makes the path of life an easier and more beautiful journey. It takes a rare combination of many qualities.

It takes a certain kind of person to be special.

It takes someone ...exactly like you.

A Little Note
with a Lot of Love

Sometimes we need reminders
in our lives
of how much people care.

If you ever get that feeling,
*   I want you to remember this...*

Beyond words that can even begin
to tell you how much,
*   I hold you and your happiness*
*   within my heart each and*
*   every day.*

I am so grateful for you and so thankful
to the years that have given me
so much to be thankful for.

I'm Going to Be Here for You, No Matter What

When you need someone to turn to, I'll be here for you. "I will do whatever it takes and give as much as I can... to help you find your smile and get you back on steady ground again."

When you just need to talk, I will listen with my heart. And I will do my best to hear the things you may want to say, but can't quite find the words for.

I will never betray the trust you put in me. All I will do is keep on caring and doing my best to see you through. If there are decisions to be made, I may offer a direction to go in. If there are tears to be dried, I will tenderly dry them...

I want you to feel completely at ease about reaching out to me.

And don't ever forget this: You couldn't impose on me if you tried. It simply isn't possible.

Your happiness and peace of mind are so closely interwoven with mine that they are inseparable.

I will truly, deeply, and completely care about you every day. You can count on that.

I hope it will invite a little more serenity into your life to know you're not alone.

And I hope it will encourage a brighter day to shine through.

I'm not going anywhere. I promise.

Unless it's to come to your side and to hold out a hand... to you.

It's Nice to Know That Some Things Will Never Change

*No matter what is happening in
   the world.
No matter what worries or frustrations
   creep in.
No matter what glad or sad tidings
   come your way.
No matter how many bills come in
   the mail.
No matter how good or bad the news
   of the day.
No matter whether the weather is
   beautiful or not.
No matter how many times your smile
   gets lost.*

*No matter what is happening anywhere
at any time...*

*You will always be in my thoughts. And
I'll always be wishing I could find a
way to remind you... that you are so
important to me.*

*I know that life can be hard sometimes
and that the world can be a crazy place.
But I want you to remember that the
two of us will always do what we can
to make things better... and my very best
wishes will be with you today, tomorrow,
and forever.*

Maybe You Can Do This Special Favor for Me...

Whenever we're apart,
I want you to keep me in your heart
and in your mind.

Just quietly close your eyes once in a while
and imagine me here, smiling and thinking
    such thankful thoughts of you.

For I spend so many quiet moments
    of my own
thinking how much I miss you,
    how hard it is to be apart,
        and how wonderful it is
        that you're always with me,
            here in my heart.

Special People

The special people in this world are the most precious and the most appreciated people of all. No matter what happens, they always understand. They go a million miles out of their way. They hold your hand.

They bring you smiles when a smile is exactly what you need. They listen, and they hear what is said in the spaces between the words.

They care, and they let you know you're in their prayers.

Special people always know the perfect thing to do. They can make your whole day just by saying something that no one else could have said. Sometimes you feel like they share with you a secret language that others can't tune in to. They can guide you, inspire you, comfort you, and light up your life with laughter...

Special people understand your moods and nurture your needs, and they lovingly know just what you're after.

When your feelings come from deep inside and they need to be spoken to someone you don't have to hide from, you share them... with special people. When good news comes, special people are the first ones you turn to. And when feelings overflow and tears need to fall, special people help you through it all.

Special people bring sunlight into your life. They warm your world with their presence, whether they are far away or close by your side.

Special people are gifts
that bring such happiness,
and they're treasures
that money can't buy.

I'm So Thankful
That You're a Part
of My Life

"Gratitude" is one of the nicest feelings a heart can have. It's a feeling that comes along for a very special reason — and it's a lovely thought that never goes away once it enters in. It joins together with precious memories and grateful hopes. Gratitude lives on, not for just a moment or a day, but through all the seasons that lie ahead.

My "thank you" feelings are especially sweet ones... when it comes to thinking of all the things you do. You deserve to receive so many smiles, such an abundance of joys, and so much generosity — reflected right back at you. That's why...

I hope you'll always remember my appreciation for everything you've done ...and my endless gratitude.

I Don't Know What I'd Do Without You

To you:

For keeping my spirits up.
For never letting me down.
For being here for me.
For knowing I'm there for you.

For bringing so many smiles my way.
For being sensitive to my needs.
For knowing just what to say.
For listening better than anyone else.

For bringing me laughter.
For bringing me light.
For understanding so much about me.
For trusting me with so much about you.

For being the best.
For being so beautiful.

> *I don't know what I'd do*
> *...without you.*

The Goodness You Give

This is for you, for being someone whose soul is so inspiring. This is a "thank you" for having a heart that's so big and a mind that is so open. And a spirit that I really love.

It's a message of gratitude for an incredibly special person. You inspire me with your wonderfulness. You're the first person I think of whenever I have something to share, and...

...you're the last person in the universe I would hurt or ever be unkind to. You are a treasure to my life, and I value you so much. You have an amazing knack for reassuring me.

You invite me to go along to the places your journeys take you when you dream, when you wonder, and when you reminisce...

And you let me know that you're a willing traveling companion, happy to join me in all my journeys, too.

I love that about you. I cherish the fact that you understand me so well and that I know you just about as well as I could ever know anyone.

*I am blessed by the thousands of smiles
we have shared, by the laughter that
lingers in my heart, and by our concerns
that have found a place of comfort in
the sanctuary of our caring. I truly
don't know what I'd do... without the
goodness you give my life.*

Everyone Needs Someone
like You

*Everyone needs someone who is
always there and always caring.
Everyone needs someone who is just a
touch or a card or a phone call away —
someone with whom you can share
everything that's in your heart
or simply talk about the day
in the way that only the two of you can.*

Everyone needs someone to encourage them,
to believe in them, to give a pat on
the back when things have gone right
and a shoulder to cry on when they haven't.
Everyone needs someone to remind them
to keep trying and that it will all work out.

I hope everyone has someone
who's as wonderful as you.

Thank You
for These Feelings

For bringing me happiness
as though it were a gift
I could open every day
...I am grateful to you.

For listening to the words
I want to say
...I appreciate you.

For letting me share the most
   personal parts of your world
   and for welcoming me with
      your eyes
         ...I am indebted to you.

For being the wonderful, kind,
   giving person you are
      ...I admire you.

For being everything you are to me
   and for doing it so beautifully,
      I thank you...
         with all my heart.

Such a Blessing

In the course of a person's lifetime, there are so many prayers that get whispered and so many hopes that fill the heart. There are wishing stars that spend their entire evenings listening to all the things we long for.

I have said those prayers and had those hopes and chatted with more than my share of stars in the sky.

I always feel that if I ask and believe and wish well enough, some things are bound to turn out right.

But in all my prayers and wishes and hopes, I couldn't have asked for
  a blessing
    more wonderful
      than you in my life.

You Touch My Life

*It seems like I'm always searching
for a way to tell you
how wonderful I think you are.*

*And I thought that maybe
this book could help me
convey a few thoughts
   that I would love to share with you...*

You're my definition of a special person.

I think you're fantastic.
And exceptional and unique and endearing.
To me, you're someone
who is very necessary to my well-being.
In so many ways, you fill my life
with happiness and the sweet feelings
of being so grateful and appreciative
*   that you're here.*

I could go on and on...
*   but you get the picture.*

I think you're a masterpiece.

A Place in My Heart

*There will always be a special place in my heart...
for you.*

*It is a place that knows how very much there
is to appreciate about you. About your giving
and your sharing. About your beautiful spirit
and your kind and caring soul. About the
generous way you manage to brighten so
many days.*

*It is a place that recognizes your uniqueness
and that celebrates the meaning of all this. It is
a place that inspires a more positive outlook
on everything every time I think of you.*

*Within my heart is a place that is filled with
warm and thankful feelings...*
   *feelings that understand how seldom
      someone like you comes along.*

Thoughts for You

*One of the most special places in my heart
   will always be saved for you.
You...
   the one person I can always talk to;
   the one person who understands.
You...
   for making me laugh in the rain;
   for helping me shoulder my troubles.*

You...
    for loving me in spite of myself
    and always putting me
        back on my feet again.
You...
    for giving me someone to believe in;
    someone who lets me know that
    there really is goodness and kindness
    and laughter and love in the world.
You...
    for being one of the best
    parts of my life and proving it
        over and over again.

In This World

There are a few absolute gems in this world. They are the people who make a tremendous difference in other people's lives... with the smiles they give, the blessings they share, and the way they warm the hearts of everyone around them.

Those rare and remarkable people are so deserving of every hope and happiness. They are the people who are incredibly unique, enormously thanked, and endlessly appreciated for everything they do.

And one of those wonderful, deserving, and one-of-a-kind people is most definitely... you.

Just Between Us

I don't think it would be possible for me to be more thankful or more appreciative of all that you are.

You are such a nice part of my life!

If it weren't for you, I wouldn't have half as much laughter or nearly as much joy...

I wouldn't have as much peace or understanding. And I definitely wouldn't have as much fun!

I love that you're here. And whether it's in person or on the phone... I love the connection that is always there between us.

What we share is really something special. I feel more at home with you than I do with just about anyone, and feelings like those are some of the most precious of all.

How Blessed I Am
to Have You in My Life

If you could see yourself reflected in my eyes, you would see someone who makes my heart just smile inside. You would catch a glimpse of somebody who has been such a wonderful influence on my life and who keeps on making a beautiful difference in my days.

If you could hear the words I would love to share, you would be able to listen to a special tribute to you, one that sings your praises, speaks of an unending gratitude, and describes how much I'll always appreciate you.

If you could imagine one of the nicest gifts anyone could ever receive, you would begin to understand what your presence in my life has meant to me.

I Wish for You

Happiness. Deep down within.

Serenity. With each sunrise.

Success. In each facet of your life.

Close and caring friends.

Love. That never ends.

Special memories. Of all the yesterdays.

A bright today. With so much to be thankful for.

A path. That leads to beautiful tomorrows.

Dreams. That do their best to come true.

*And appreciation. Of all the wonderful
   things about you.*

You Are a
Very Special Person

*I want you to know how amazing you are.
I want you to know how much you're
treasured and celebrated and quietly thanked.*

*I want you to feel really good...
    about who you are.
About all the great things you do!*

*I want you to appreciate your uniqueness.
Acknowledge your talents and abilities.
Realize what a beautiful soul you have.
Understand the wonder within...*

*You make so much sun shine through, and
you inspire so much joy in the lives of
everyone who is lucky enough to know you.*

*You are a very special person, giving so
many people a reason to smile...*

You deserve to receive the best in return, and one of my heart's favorite hopes is that the happiness you give away will come back to warm you each and every day of your life.

I Think the World of You

Do you know what you are? You are one of the most special people I will ever have the privilege of knowing.

I really mean that. The older I get, the more I understand how rare it is to be blessed with someone like you...

You're unique in so many ways, and there are very few things in life that even come close to bringing me as much happiness as you do.

You never cease to amaze me. There are so many moments when I am quietly in awe of you... of the joy you inspire, of the serenity you share, and of all the great things that just seem to naturally be a part of you.

It's so easy and so nice... being with you. It opens my eyes to all the wonderful qualities about you. I see goodness and kindness there. I see compassion and understanding.

And I never fail to see a twinkle in your eyes... a gentle reminder to me that I am in the company of someone who has a big heart and a beautiful ability to make each day a good one...

I know you're probably going to feel a little embarrassed to hear all the praises I am singing about you, but you deserve all these praises... and many, many more. I'll always think the world of you.

I'll cherish all the memories and appreciate the closeness and thank my lucky stars for everything.

So please... don't ever forget:

*I think you are one of the
most precious people
this world will ever be
blessed with.*

About the Author

Best-selling author and editor Douglas Pagels has inspired millions of readers with his insights and his anthologies. No one is better at touching on so many subjects that are deeply personal and truly universal at the same time.

His writings have been translated into over a dozen languages due to their global appeal and inspiring outlook on life, and his work has been quoted by many worthy causes and charitable organizations.

He and his wife live in Colorado, and they are the parents of children in college and beyond. Over the years, Doug has spent much of his time as a classroom volunteer, a youth basketball coach, an advocate for local environmental issues, a frequent traveler, and a craftsman, building a cabin in the Rocky Mountains.